The Reconstruction Era

By
CINDY BARDEN

ISBN 1-58037-187-6

Printing No. CD-1533

Mark Twain Media, Inc., Publishers
Distributed by Carson-Dellosa Publishing Company, Inc.

Table of Contents

About the American History Series

Welcome to *The Reconstruction Era,* one of 12 books in the Mark Twain Media, Inc., American History series for students in grades four to seven.

The activity books in this series are designed as stand-alone material for classrooms and home-schoolers or as supplemental material to enhance your history curriculum. Students also can be encouraged to use the books as independent study units to improve their understanding of historical events and people.

Each book provides challenging activities that enable students to explore history, geography, and social studies topics. The activities provide research opportunities and promote critical reading, thinking, and writing skills. As students follow the progress of Reconstruction after the Civil War and learn about the people and events that influenced history, they will draw conclusions; write opinions; compare and contrast historical events, people, and places; analyze cause and effect; and improve mapping skills. Students will also have the opportunity to apply what they learn to their own lives through reflection and creative writing.

Students can further increase their knowledge and understanding of historical events by using reference sources at the library and on the Internet. Students may need assistance to learn how to use search engines and discover appropriate websites.

Titles of books for additional reading appropriate to the subject matter at this grade level are included in each book.

Although many of the questions are open-ended, an answer key is included at the back of the book for questions with specific answers.

Share a journey through history with your students as you explore the books in the Mark Twain Media, Inc., American History series:

Discovering and Exploring the Americas
Life in the Colonies
The American Revolution
The Lewis and Clark Expedition
The Westward Movement
The California Gold Rush
The Oregon and Santa Fe Trails
Slavery in the United States
The American Civil War
Abraham Lincoln and His Times
The Reconstruction Era
Industrialization in America

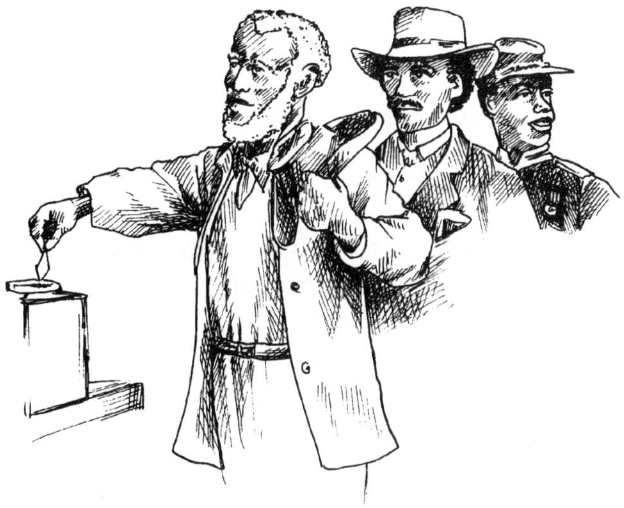

Time Line of *The Reconstruction Era* (1865–1877)

1865 **March 3:** Congress established the Freedmen's Bureau.
March 4: Lincoln began his second term as president.
April 9: The Civil War ended when General Lee surrendered.
April 14: Lincoln was assassinated by John Wilkes Booth.
April 15: Andrew Johnson became president.
December 18: The Thirteenth Amendment abolished slavery.

1866 **February 19:** The new Freedmen's Bureau Bill was passed.
April 9: The Civil Rights Act was passed.
May 1: The Memphis race riot occurred.
July 30: The New Orleans race riot occurred.

1867 **January 8:** Black citizens in Washington, D.C., were granted the right to vote.
March 1: Nebraska became a state.
March 2: The first Reconstruction Act was passed.
March 2: The Tenure of Office Act was passed.
April: Alaska was purchased from Russia for $7.2 million in gold.

1868 Arkansas, Alabama, Florida, Louisiana, and North and South Carolina were readmitted to the Union.
February 24: Congress voted to impeach Andrew Johnson.
March 23: President Johnson's impeachment trial began.
May 16: President Johnson was acquitted.
July 28: The Fourteenth Amendment was passed.
November 3: Ulysses S. Grant was elected president.
December 25: Unconditional amnesty was granted by presidential proclamation to all participants in the "insurrection or rebellion" against the United States.

1870 Georgia, Mississippi, Texas, and Virginia were readmitted as states.
February 25: The first Black U.S. senator entered Congress.
March 30: The Fifteenth Amendment was passed.
June 27: Congress established the Department of Justice.

1871 **February 28:** The Federal Election Law was passed.

1872 **November 5:** President Grant was reelected.

1875 **March 1:** The Civil Rights Act granted Blacks equal rights in public places and allowed them to serve on juries.

1876 **December 6:** Rutherford B. Hayes was elected president by electoral vote.

1877 **June 15:** Henry O. Fipper became the first Black American to graduate from the U.S. Military Academy at West Point.

Name: ____________________ Date: ____________

What Was Reconstruction?

When the American Civil War ended in 1865, the South was in shambles. The Union Army had destroyed homes, businesses, farm animals, and fields. The Southern economy was ruined. The social system that had existed in the South before the Civil War had been destroyed. Over 250,000 Confederate soldiers had been killed.

With the Confederate government powerless, the North clearly had to deal with the situation. The plan for rebuilding the South and reuniting it with the Union was known as **Reconstruction** (1865–1877).

Most Northerners believed that Reconstruction was necessary because of conditions in the Southern states, but few agreed on what should be done. They also disagreed about how to ensure the freedom and civil rights of former slaves. Reconstruction caused one of the greatest disputes in the United States. People today still argue about it.

Even though there were many different ideas about how Reconstruction should be handled, most of the debates involved two opposing viewpoints: the **radical** approach favored by Congress and the **moderate** approach proposed by President Abraham Lincoln.

1. Why do you think the North felt it was up to them to come up with a plan for Reconstruction?

____

____

2. Congress felt that the South should pay a high price for its disloyalty. Do you agree or disagree? Explain your answer. Use your own paper if you need more room.

____

____

____

3. On your own paper, draw a political cartoon to show the Radical point of view to Reconstruction.

Name: ______________________ Date: ______________

The Issue of Slavery

Many people think of White Southerners before the Civil War as slave owners living on large plantations with hundreds of slaves. However, this wasn't actually the case. Seventy-five percent of Southern families didn't own any slaves. Only about 30,000 Southerners owned 50 or more slaves.

Those who owned large plantations and hundreds of slaves were, of course, the most wealthy, the ones most likely to be well educated, and the ones most likely to run for and be elected to political offices. They were also the ones most often mentioned in history books.

Most Southerners who owned only a few slaves lived and worked on smaller farms and in cities. Slaves also worked in shipyards, in businesses, in stores, and in homes.

Slavery had existed for thousands of years before it came to the American colonies. In most cases, slaves were prisoners of war or people who were made slaves for a specific period of time because of a crime they had committed or a debt they owed.

In the United States, unlike other parts of the world, slavery came to be based on only one criteria—race. Slavery was inherited through the mother. Any child born to a female slave was automatically a slave.

Slave owners believed their slaves were not human beings. Slaves were property and had no more rights than their horses, dogs, or riding boots.

1. Why do you think little is written about people in the South who didn't own slaves or who owned only a few slaves?

____

____

____

2. Do you think it was morally right to make slaves of people who had committed a crime, owed a debt, or were prisoners of war? Why or why not?

____

____

____

3. Why do you think slavery in the United States was different from the way it was in other countries?

____

____

4. What do you think about slaves being treated like property? ______________

____

____

Name: ______________________ Date: ______________

Lincoln's Ten Percent Plan

Abraham Lincoln

The Civil War began with the Battle at Fort Sumter in 1861. Eleven states broke away from the Union and formed their own country, the Confederate States of America.

The Civil War continued much longer than anyone expected. It did not end until General Lee surrendered to General Grant on April 9, 1865.

Even before the Civil War ended, however, people talked about what would happen when the country was again at peace. How would the Confederate States be reunited with the United States? What penalties should be imposed on the people of the states that had seceded?

President Lincoln had a simple plan for reuniting the nation. Known as the "Ten Percent Plan," it required that ten percent of the voters in a state that had joined the Confederacy must take an oath of loyalty to the United States. Then the state could send representatives to Congress, and the state would be readmitted to the Union.

Northerners who supported Lincoln's plan were called moderates. They, like Lincoln, believed that the Southern states should not be harshly punished for seceding from the Union and should be readmitted as quickly as possible.

Lincoln looked forward to "a just and lasting peace." His goal was to help both sides recover and rebuild. At his first public appearance after the war, Lincoln asked the band to play "Dixie," a favorite Southern song. "I have always thought 'Dixie' one of the best tunes I have ever heard," he said.

Unfortunately, Lincoln was assassinated before he could implement his plan.

1. If a state had one million voting citizens, how many would have to take the oath of loyalty for the state to be readmitted? ______________________

2. Do you think Lincoln's plan was a good one? Why or why not? ______________________

____

____

____

____

3. Using the Internet or other reference sources, find the words to the song, "Dixie." Play a recording of the song, or perhaps someone in the class with a musical instrument could perform the song.

Name: ____________________ Date: __________

The Thirteenth Amendment

When Abraham Lincoln issued the Emancipation Proclamation on January 1, 1863, he freed slaves in all states or parts of states in rebellion against the United States—about one million slaves.

However, this did not include freedom for the three million slaves in states that had not seceded from the Union or even in certain areas of states that had seceded.

1. Use a dictionary. Define *emancipation.* ____________________

2. How do you think slaves who were freed by the Emancipation Proclamation felt about Lincoln?

3. What percent of slaves had not been freed? ____________________

4. How do you think slaves who were not freed by the Emancipation Proclamation felt about Lincoln?

5. Why do you think Lincoln did not abolish slavery everywhere in the United States?

☆☆☆☆☆☆☆☆☆☆☆☆☆☆☆☆☆☆☆☆☆☆☆☆☆

Amendment 13

Section 1. Neither slavery nor involuntary servitude, except as punishment for crime whereof the party shall have been duly convicted, shall exist within the United States, or any place subject to their jurisdiction.

☆☆☆☆☆☆☆☆☆☆☆☆☆☆☆☆☆☆☆☆☆☆☆☆☆

In December 1865, the Thirteenth Amendment to the Constitution of the United States finally freed all slaves within the United States and made slavery illegal forever. It also gave Congress the power to enforce this amendment.

However, Southern Blacks now faced the difficulty Northern Blacks had confronted—that of freedmen surrounded by hostile Whites. One freedman, Houston Hartsfield Holloway, wrote, "For we colored people did not know how to be free, and the White people did not know how to have a free colored person about them."

Name: ______________________________ Date: ______________

Andrew Johnson's Early Life

Andrew Johnson was a successful tailor in his shop in Greeneville, Tennessee.

Andrew Johnson was only three years old when his father died. His mother worked hard to support her two sons, but there was never enough money. Schooling for the two boys cost money and was out of the question.

Even after his mother remarried, they had little money. "If being poor was a crime," Johnson once said, "I should have to plead that I was guilty."

In 1822, Johnson's mother arranged for 13-year-old Andrew and his brother to become apprentice tailors. In exchange for food and clothing, he and his brother worked for the tailor and learned the trade.

When he was 16, Andrew, his brother, and some other boys played a prank on a woman. When she threatened to have them arrested, Andrew and his brother ran away. In spite of a $10 reward offered for their return, the boys stayed away for over a year. When Andrew returned, he apologized, but the tailor refused to take him back.

Deciding it was time for a change, Andrew, his mother, brother, and stepfather loaded their belongings into a two-wheeled wooden cart pulled by an old horse and began their journey west.

When they arrived in Greeneville, Tennessee, it seemed like a good place to settle. Andrew got a job as a tailor and met Eliza McCardle, the daughter of a shoemaker who had died a few years earlier. They were married in 1827. Although he could read a little, he didn't know how to write his own name.

Johnson opened his own tailor shop. While he worked, his wife read to him. In the evenings, she taught him to write and do simple arithmetic. The man who later became the President of the United States never forgot his humble beginnings.

Use a dictionary.

1. Define *apprentice.* ______________________________
2. Define *tailor.* ______________________________
3. On your own paper, compare Andrew Johnson's early life and education to Abraham Lincoln's.

Name: ______________________________ Date: ________________

Johnson's Early Political Career

As Johnson's tailoring business grew, he became more prosperous. He bought a house for his family and a building for his business. He hired assistant tailors and purchased eight slaves.

He won his first election at the age of 19 when he was elected village alderman of Greeneville, Tennessee. Two years later, he was elected village mayor.

In 1835, Johnson won election to the state legislature. Always keeping the needs of farmers and common people in mind, Johnson voted against what he considered wasteful government spending. He refused to approve money to improve state roads and funds for a railroad. Those two decisions cost him the next election.

By moderating his views on "internal improvements," he was reelected several more times to the state legislature and then to the U.S. House of Representatives in 1843. Often Johnson upheld the views of most Southerners, including the belief that slavery was necessary for the Southern economy.

Johnson was not afraid to side with the North, however, or even take an independent view when he believed he was right. His refusal to always side with the Southerners earned him praise from many Northern Congressmen but also many political enemies in the South.

After serving ten years in the House, his opponents found a way to prevent him from being reelected by changing the boundaries of his district to include more voters who didn't approve of Johnson's politics.

Although their tactics caused him to lose the election for the Senate, he ran for and was elected governor of Tennessee in 1853.

1. Do you think it likely that a person who was 19 and had almost no education could be elected to any office today? Why or why not? Explain on your own paper.

2. Since Johnson wasn't a plantation owner or farmer, why do you think he believed slavery was necessary?

____

____

____

3. How do you think Johnson's opponents felt when he became governor of Tennessee?

____

____

Name:______________________________ Date:______________

Andrew Johnson Becomes President

The governor of Kentucky, who had once been a blacksmith, made a shovel and tongs and sent them to Johnson as a symbolic gift. Johnson returned the favor by sewing a suit for the Kentucky governor.

Throughout Johnson's political career, his popularity was with the common men of the state. His wealthy political opponents ridiculed his humble origins and lack of formal education.

"Some day I will show the stuck-up aristocrats who is running the country," Johnson once said. "They are ... not as good as the man who earns his bread by the sweat of his brow."

As governor of Tennessee, Johnson established the state's first public school system and founded the state's first public library.

After two terms as governor, Johnson was elected to the U.S. Senate. When the Southern states formed the Confederacy, Johnson was the only Southern senator who refused to give up his seat in Congress. Johnson blamed the Civil War and secession on wealthy White plantation owners.

"I shall stay inside the Union and there fight for Southern rights. I advise all others to do the same."

Many Northerners applauded Johnson for supporting the Union. When Lincoln ran for his second term of office in 1864, he invited Johnson to be his running mate.

After Lincoln was assassinated, Andrew Johnson became president.

1. On your own paper, decide whether you agree or disagree with Johnson about the aristocrats not being as good as the common people? Why? Explain your answer.

2. What do you think the gifts between the two governors symbolized? ______________

____

3. Considering Johnson's lack of formal education, why do you think his efforts to establish a public school system and public libraries were important to him?

____

____

____

4. Why do you think Johnson chose to remain in the Senate even though all other Southern senators resigned?

____

____

____

Name: ______________________ Date: ______________

Learn More About Andrew Johnson

Use the Internet or other reference sources to answer these questions about Andrew Johnson.

1. When and where was Andrew Johnson born? ______________________________

____

2. What "prank" did he and the other boys play that caused the Johnson brothers to run away from home because they feared they would be arrested?

____

____

____

3. What was Andrew Johnson's brother's name?

____

4. How many children did Andrew and Eliza Johnson have, and what were their names?

____

____

5. To what position did Abraham Lincoln appoint Andrew Johnson in 1861 after the Civil War began?

____

6. What happened to the Johnsons' home during the Civil War? ______________________

____

7. The plot to assassinate Abraham Lincoln also included a plan to kill the vice president and other top government officials. Who was the man assigned to kill Andrew Johnson?

____

8. After his term of office as president ended, what election did Johnson win?

____

9. When, where, and how did Andrew Johnson die? ______________________________

____

10. On your own paper, write a paragraph summarizing what you think about Andrew Johnson as a person.

Name: ______________________________ Date: ______________

Reconstruction Under President Johnson

Shortly after Johnson became president, Congress recessed for the summer. Northern Radicals expected Johnson to continue to support their plans for Reconstruction. However, Johnson did not favor equal rights for Blacks. He believed that "White men alone must manage the South." Johnson offered Blacks no role in Reconstruction.

Johnson's plan for Reconstruction was even more liberal than Lincoln's. He required only that the Southern states agree that slavery and secession were illegal.

Once that was done, they were allowed to elect their own leaders and members of Congress. Johnson believed only Whites should be allowed to vote and encouraged the Southern states to rejoin the Union as quickly as possible.

Since freedmen were not allowed to vote, many former Confederate leaders, including the former Confederate vice president, were elected to high positions in the South and in Congress.

In the summer of 1865, Johnson pardoned hundreds of former Rebel soldiers. His pardon was automatic except for those who were wealthy. Having grown up poor, Johnson always resented those who had money. Anyone with assets of $20,000 or more had to apply in person to receive a pardon. By the summer of 1866, Johnson had pardoned almost everyone.

With the former leaders of the Southern states back in control, the states passed laws known as the Black Codes, which were designed to keep former slaves in conditions very close to slavery. Violence and racism were common.

When Congress went back into session in December 1865, those who had hoped for a peaceful and quick Reconstruction were alarmed by Johnson's policies. Northern members refused to allow Southerners to participate in Congress until their states had been readmitted to the Union. They criticized the way President Johnson had handled Reconstruction.

Johnson demanded the recognition of congressmen from the South and declared that Reconstruction was finished.

1. Who do you think was right: President Johnson or Congress? Why? ______________

____

____

____

____

2. Use a dictionary. Define *freedman.* ______________________________

____

3. How do you think those who had fought in the Union Army felt about President Johnson pardoning most of the Rebel soldiers?

____

____

____

Name: ______________________________ Date: ________________

The Black Codes of 1865 and 1866

After the Civil War, newly-freed slaves soon learned that freedom was not what they expected it to be. Many of the former Confederate states passed laws known as the Black Codes. These laws were based on the slave codes that had been in effect since early colonial days.

The Black Codes were intended to keep the social situation in the South as close as possible to what it had been before the Civil War. Even though slaves were legally free, they were allowed very little freedom.

The Black Codes were designed to continue providing cheap sources of labor for White Southerners and were based on the belief that Blacks were inferior beings. Blacks were required to sign yearly labor contracts, often with their former masters.

Blacks who were unemployed and without a permanent residence could be declared vagrants. Vagrants were arrested and fined. If unable to pay, they were forced to work to pay off the fine.

Some states limited the types of property freedmen could own and where they could live. They were excluded from certain businesses or from specific trades in some states. Former slaves were not allowed to carry firearms, meet in unsupervised groups, or testify in court against Whites. Freedmen could not vote or hold public office. They had to receive permission to travel and were forbidden to live in many cities. They were allowed to marry, but interracial marriage was strictly forbidden.

The harsh Black Codes and treatment of freedmen by Southern Whites were part of the reason Congress took such a radical view of Reconstruction. The situation in the South also prompted the passage of the Fourteenth and Fifteenth Amendments to the Constitution.

Reconstruction eliminated the Black Codes, but many of the restrictions of the Black Codes became legal again under a series of Jim Crow laws. Some of these laws were not abolished until passage of the Civil Rights Act of 1964.

1. Use a dictionary. Define *vagrant.* ______________________________

   ____

2. Why do you think White people in the South continued to treat freedmen this way?

   ____

   ____

   ____

3. What was the difference beween the freedom the newly-freed slaves expected and what actually happened?

   ____

   ____

   ____

Name: ______________________________ Date: ______________

Carl Schurz Reports to the President

Carl Schurz

Carl Schurz, a German immigrant, passed his bar exam in Milwaukee, Wisconsin, in 1859. He became a close friend of Abraham Lincoln who appointed him U.S. Minister to Spain in 1861. After serving in the Union Army during the Civil War, he became a journalist.

After the war, President Andrew Johnson sent Carl Schurz to the South to report on conditions firsthand. He wanted to know how well Reconstruction was working and the actual status of freedmen.

Schurz spent months touring the South, talking to army personnel, Southern leaders, and common people, both Black and White. Everywhere he went, he found similar problems.

Most former slaves were trying to start new lives. They wanted to own homes, hold good jobs, and provide education for themselves and their children.

Schurz found that for the most part, however, the attitudes of Southerners had not changed. In spite of the Emancipation Proclamation, they still viewed Blacks as property, not people. Some plantation owners kept their former slaves nearby, living in the same places, working in the same fields, doing the same jobs they had done when they were slaves. Schurz reported that Blacks were attacked, their schools, churches, and homes burned, and their rights denied.

In spite of Schurz's report, President Johnson continued his Reconstruction policies.

1. Why do you think President Johnson sent Carl Schurz to report on conditions in the South if he didn't plan on making any changes based on the report?

____

____

____

____

2. What effect do you think Schurz's report had on Northern Radicals? ______________

____

____

____

Name: ______________________________ Date: ______________

The Freedmen's Bureau

After Lincoln issued the Emancipation Proclamation, thousands of former slaves, called freedmen, ran away from their owners. Most had no property, few skills, no education, and nowhere to go.

The U.S. Bureau of Refugees, Freedmen, and Abandoned Lands was established by Congress on March 3, 1865, to provide health care, education, and assistance to freedmen. By the time the Civil War ended, the bureau had opened offices throughout the South and had begun providing relief to both Blacks and Whites.

Besides providing aid to four million Black Americans, the Freedmen's Bureau opened more than 1,000 schools for Blacks and spent over $400,000 to establish teacher training centers. It opened hospitals and provided medical assistance to over a million people.

In February 1866, Congress wanted to give the bureau more power to defend freedmen against the Black Codes. President Johnson vetoed the bill. Johnson declared that states should have the right to make their own laws and the federal government shouldn't interfere. Congress overrode the President's veto and passed the Freedmen's Bill on February 19, 1866.

Although it did much to help Southern Blacks, the bureau had inadequate funds and poorly-trained personnel. As more and more of the power was drained away from this agency, it eventually did little more than oversee sharecropping arrangements. Congress terminated the bureau in July 1872.

1. Use a dictionary. Define *veto.* ______________________________

2. Do you agree or disagree with Johnson that states should have the right to make their own laws without federal interference? Why?

____

____

____

3. How do you think Northern members of Congress felt about Johnson's veto?

____

____

____

Name: ______________________ Date: ______________

How Congress Passes Laws

Article I of the U.S. Constitution established the way new laws are introduced and approved.

A proposed law is first introduced as a bill, usually in the House of Representatives. Members of both branches of Congress discuss the bill. At that point it may be rewritten. A majority of members of both the Senate and the House must approve the bill before it is sent to the president for approval.

The president has several choices.

A. If the president approves and signs the bill within ten days, it becomes a law.

B. If the president objects to the bill, he can return it to the house in which it originated within ten days with an explanation of his objections. This is called a **veto**.

1. Then the House and Senate can either change the bill and resubmit it to the president for approval or take another vote on the original bill.

2. If two-thirds of the members of both the Senate and House of Representatives vote to pass the original bill, it becomes a law even without the president's approval. This is called **overriding a veto**.

C. If the president does not sign the bill within ten days and does not return it to Congress, it automatically becomes a law unless Congress has adjourned.

While he was president, Andrew Johnson vetoed 29 bills; Congress overrode 15 of them.

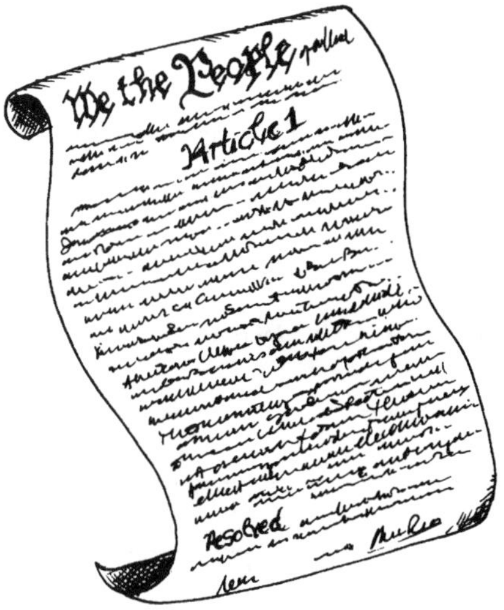

Fill in the blanks.

1. The ______________________ established how new laws are made.
2. When Congress feels a new law is needed, a ______________________ is introduced.
3. A ______________________ of members of the Senate and House of Representatives must approve the bill before it goes to the president.
4. If the president does not agree to sign a bill, he can return it to Congress within ______________________ days.
5. Then ______________________ of the members of both the Senate and House must vote to approve a bill for it to become a law.

Name: ______________________________ Date: ________________

No Homes for the Homeless

General William T. Sherman

In January 1865, General Sherman issued Special Field Order No. 15, setting aside abandoned lands on the sea islands and along the cost of South Carolina and Georgia for exclusive use by freed slaves from the region.

One of the original responsibilities of the Freedmen's Bureau was to help homeless Blacks find places to live. Congressman Charles Sumner urged the government to divide up the large Southern plantations and give the land to former slaves.

President Johnson reversed General Sherman's order. As he pardoned Southerners, Johnson returned their lands to them. Even though they didn't agree with the president on most items regarding Reconstruction, Congress refused to consider any form of land redistribution.

1. Do you think Special Field Order No. 15 was a good plan? Why or why not?

____

____

____

2. What is your opinion of Charles Sumner's plan? Was it a good idea? Why or why not?

____

____

____

3. How do you think the South would have reacted if this plan had been followed?

____

____

____

4. Why do you think Congress would not consider any form of land redistribution?

____

____

____

5. On your own paper, explain whether or not you think it was fair to allow the Southerners who had joined the Confederacy to retain their land and property. Why or why not?

Name: ______________________________ Date: ______________

What If?

1. What if you had been a member of a congressional committee in 1865 assigned to recommend guidelines for readmitting the Southern states? List three or more requirements you think would have been fair and a reason for each.

2. What if you had been a former Confederate leader and were asked for your opinion of what would be fair guidelines for readmitting the Southern states? List three or more requirements and a reason for each.

3. Write a "What if?" question about the Reconstruction Era and answer it.

Question: ______________________________

Answer: ______________________________

Name: ____________________ Date: ____________

Southern Congressmen Turned Away

Thaddeus Stevens

Congress did not meet for regular sessions between May and December 1865. During that time, President Johnson had a free hand to implement his Reconstruction policies. He quickly readmitted all the former Confederate states except Texas to the Union.

When Congress met in December, they were amazed and outraged to find that the South had elected men who had led the fight against the Union only six months earlier as new members to Congress.

The number of members a state has in the U.S. House of Representatives is based on population. Previously, Blacks had only been counted as three-fifths of a person. Now that they were freed, each Black was counted as a whole person. That change meant that the South would have at least 12 more representatives in Congress.

As a result, the Northern Republicans would no longer be able to control policies regarding the South, and the Southerners were back in Congress, stronger than ever.

Although it was dishonest and unfair, Radical Republicans disqualified the Southern congressmen; then they appointed a committee to study the matter. Of course, the committee consisted only of Radical Republicans.

Led by Thaddeus Stevens, this group became known as the Committee of Fifteen. They were in charge not only of deciding the issue of allowing the Southern congressmen to participate but also of Reconstruction policies in general. They studied the problem for several months.

When Congress did act, it passed a series of laws that changed the requirements for Southern states to be readmitted to the Union. Until those requirements were met, the Radical Republicans had a valid reason for refusing to allow Southern congressmen to participate.

To further strengthen their position, the Radicals added Section 3 to the Fourteenth Amendment, prohibiting anyone who had held office or been a leader of the Confederacy from voting or being elected.

1. What do you think of the tactic of the Radical Republicans of forming a committee to study the situation?

   ____

   ____

2. Why do you think it took so long for the committee to make a decision?

   ____

   ____

Name:______________________________ Date:______________

The Civil Rights Act of 1866

In March 1866, Congress passed another bill called the Civil Rights Act. This bill gave freedmen their civil rights and promised protection of their rights. It conferred citizenship upon Black men and guaranteed them equal rights with Whites.

Again President Johnson vetoed the bill. For the second time, Congress overrode Johnson's veto, making the bill a law in April 1866.

When Johnson learned that Congress had overridden his veto, he claimed that Congress was filled with traitors. Congress, led by Northern Radicals, came up with their own plan for Reconstruction.

Thaddeus Stevens, a leader of the Radical Republicans, stated: "Every man, no matter what his race or color … has an equal right to justice, honesty, fair play with every other man; and the law should secure him those rights …"

Although the Civil Rights Act granted citizenship and civil rights to Black men, Congress felt it was necessary to make the law even stronger by writing another amendment to the Constitution in June. They sent it to the states for approval.

President Johnson publicly attacked this amendment and convinced all the former Confederate states, except Tennessee, to reject it. Delaware and Kentucky also failed to approve it. His actions caused a two-year delay before the amendment was finally approved. In the meantime, the gulf between the president and Congress grew wider.

The situation in the South grew worse. Violence increased. A White mob in Memphis, Tennessee, killed 47 Blacks and destroyed homes, schools, and churches. During a political meeting of Blacks in New Orleans, a mob of White policemen and firemen attacked the demonstrators. Of the 48 people killed, most were Blacks.

1. Do you agree with Stevens' statement? Why or why not? ______________________________

____

____

____

2. What is your opinion of President Johnson's attitude and actions? ______________________

____

____

____

Name: ____________________ Date: ____________

The Congressional Plan

Lincoln and Johnson's plans for Reconstruction were much more lenient than the plan proposed by Congress, which involved reorganizing the Southern states, setting provisions for readmitting them into the Union, and working out a system by which Whites and Blacks could live together in a nonslave society.

Congress declared that a majority of White male citizens had to swear that they had never been disloyal to the United States.

Congress also demanded that the states would have to ratify the Fourteenth Amendment and rewrite state constitutions abolishing slavery and making secession illegal.

Northerners that supported the congressional plan were called Radicals. They claimed that the South should not be permitted to get away with treason. Lincoln had not approved of the harsh measures and had refused to sign the plan into law.

The debate was fierce, but Congress finally gained enough power to implement its plan. Congress passed a series of Reconstruction Acts dividing the South into five military districts to be in effect until the states adopted new constitutions and were readmitted to the Union. The military presence ensured that Blacks could vote without fear, and many even held political office for a short time.

Little was done to restore the South to its former economic status. As a result, the South lagged behind the North technologically, economically, and socially for many decades.

Southern Whites were outraged and humiliated by Northern military rule. They refused to accept former slaves as equals. Most people in the South saw Reconstruction as a shameful, even vengeful, imposition.

1. Use a dictionary. Define *majority.* ____________________

____

2. How many out of one million would need to take the oath of loyalty under the Congressional Plan?

____

3. What is your opinion of this Reconstruction Plan? ____________________

____

____

____

4. Which plan do you think was better: Lincoln's or the one Congress established? Why?

____

____

____

____

Name: ______________________________ Date: ______________

Many Questions Needed Answers

Federal leaders had to try to answer many questions when they formed their policies for Reconstruction.

- What should be the relationship between the North and the South once the Civil War ended?
- What should be demanded from the Confederate States before they were allowed to rejoin the Union?
- What needed to be accomplished before Reconstruction could be considered complete in a Southern state?
- Who was responsible for the Confederate rebellion and who, if anyone, should be punished?
- What rights should newly-freed slaves have, and how should those rights be guaranteed?
- What responsibility did the federal government have to ensure that freedmen received equal rights?
- How could the Southern economy be changed from one built on slave labor to one based on free labor?
- What, if any, responsibility did the federal government have for helping Southern Whites who had lost property during the war?

1. Select one of the questions. Use reference sources to learn more about the problem. On your own paper, explain what you think should have/could have been done. Give examples and reasons for your suggestions. Use the area below for notes.

____

____

____

____

____

Name: ____________________ Date: ____________

The Fourteenth Amendment

☆☆☆☆☆☆☆☆☆☆☆☆☆☆☆☆☆☆☆☆☆☆

Amendment 14

Section 1. All persons born or naturalized in the United States, and subject to the jurisdiction thereof, are citizens of the United States and of the state wherein they reside. No state shall make or enforce any law which shall abridge the privileges or immunities of citizens of the United States; nor shall any state deprive any person of life, liberty, or property, without due process of law; nor deny to any person within its jurisdiction the equal protection of the laws.

☆☆☆☆☆☆☆☆☆☆☆☆☆☆☆☆☆☆☆☆☆☆☆☆☆

Adopted on July 28, 1868, the Fourteenth Amendment granted citizenship to men over 21 who had been born or naturalized in the United States. It also guaranteed **due process** (right to a trial by a jury) and equal protection under the law to all citizens.

However, even though the amendment said "all persons," it didn't mean everyone. Women and Native Americans were excluded. The exception for Native Americans is included in another section of the amendment, and the specific words "male citizens" are used to exclude women. This meant that women and Native Americans were not considered citizens and had none of the rights granted by the amendment.

Section 3 of this amendment banned everyone who formerly held office in one of the states that seceded from the Union during the Civil War from voting or holding public office. This section was designed to punish the leaders of the Confederacy and was not deleted by Congress until 1889.

1. Why do you think Native Americans were not included? ____________________

____

____

____

____

2. Why do you think women were not included? ____________________

____

____

____

3. How do you think women and Native Americans felt about this amendment?

____

____

____

Name: ____________________ Date: ____________

Payment for Freed Slaves

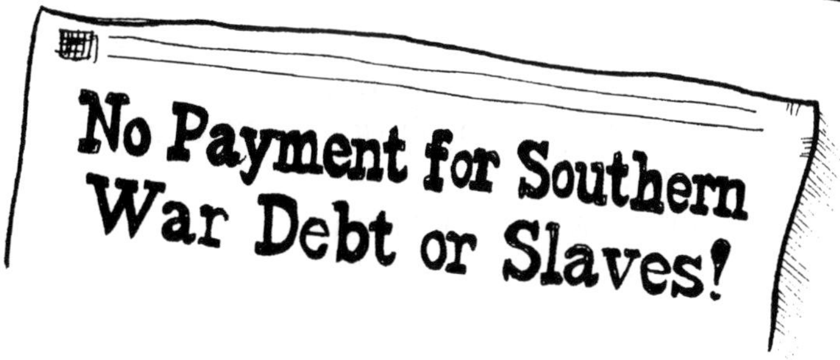

When he was a congressman, Lincoln proposed an emancipation program to free all slaves born after January 1, 1850, and enroll them in apprenticeship programs. He proposed that freeing other slaves would be voluntary. Anyone who freed his slaves voluntarily would be compensated by the government.

When the Fourteenth Amendment was written, the issue of repayment to slave-holders for their slaves was considered. The last part of section 4 addresses this.

> … neither the United States nor any state shall assume or pay any debt or obligation incurred in aid of insurrection or rebellion against the United States, or any claim for the loss of emancipation of any slave; but all such debts, obligations, and claims shall be held illegal and void.

1. Would you have voted for Lincoln's plan? Why or why not? ____________________

2. If Lincoln's plan had been approved in 1850, do you think the Civil War could have been avoided? Why or why not?

3. If Congress had offered to pay former slave owners, what do you think would have been the reaction of Northerners?

4. What do you think the reaction of Southerners would have been to an offer for payment?

5. On your own paper, write your opinion of this and why you feel this way.

Name: ______________________________ Date: ______________

Reactions in the North

When the Civil War ended, Union soldiers were glad to return to their homes and families. Many had strong feelings against the South, especially during the first few months after the war.

Some had personal reasons, like the loss of loved ones. Different people in the North had different opinions. Some of the more common ones included these:

- The Southerners had started the war in the first place by seceding from the Union, so it was all their fault.
- Rebel soldiers had killed and wounded hundreds of thousands of Northern soldiers and should be made to pay for their crimes.
- The war had cost the country millions of dollars. The South should repay the North for the cost of the war.
- The lives of millions of Northerners had been disrupted for four years while the Civil War was fought.
- Southerners did not have the right to force people into slavery. Blacks should have equal rights.

Some Northerners wanted Southerners to pay for what they believed were crimes of treason. When Andrew Johnson pardoned former Confederate leaders, some Northerners were enraged. They believed the leaders, and possibly everyone who fought in the Confederate Army, should be imprisoned or hanged.

1. Select one of the reasons why Northerners wanted revenge on the South even after the war was over. On your own paper, explain why you think they were right or wrong.

2. What do you think would have happened if the North had attempted to punish all Confederate soldiers and leaders by sending them to prison or hanging them?

____

____

____

____

____

Name:______________________________ Date:______________

Reactions in the South

Southerners had many reasons for being angry after the Civil War ended.

- Hundreds of thousands of Confederate soldiers had died and been wounded. Many were permanently disabled.
- The Southern states believed that since they had joined the Union voluntarily, they had the right to leave it if they wished to do so.
- Slaves were property. The Constitution guaranteed men the right to own property. The government did not have the right to deprive them of their property.
- The North refused to mind its own business. The war was all its fault.
- The South had been defeated in the war.
- Much of the land, crops, and property in the South had been destroyed.
- The North forced Southerners to live under military rule during Reconstruction.
- Southerners were expected to treat Blacks, whom they considered inferior beings, like equals.

In retaliation, many Southerners formed vigilante groups—secret terrorist organizations, such as the Ku Klux Klan and the Knights of the White Camelia—for the purpose of reestablishing White authority over Blacks.

The Ku Klux Klan (KKK) and other similar groups intimidated Blacks and other ethnic and religious minorities through threats and violence. Dressed in robes and masks to conceal their identities, they attacked government officials sent from the North and made night raids to terrorize Blacks.

1. Select one of the reasons why Southerners felt angry and vengeful against Northerners. On your own paper, explain why you think they were right or wrong.
2. What is your reaction to groups like the KKK? ______________________________

____

____

____

____

____

____

Name: ______________________ Date: ______________

What Would You Do?

1. You are a Confederate soldier, back from the war. You return and find your home burned down, your family living in a shed, all your farm animals killed, and your fields in ruin. What would you do?

____

____

____

2. You are a member of Congress. President Johnson vetoed a bill you believe should be passed. You respect the office of president, but feel that Johnson is wrong—again. It's your turn to make a speech in Congress. What would you do?

____

____

____

3. You are a former slave living in the South. The Civil War is over, and you are free. However, you have no place to live and no job. Your family needs food and clothing. Your former master offered you a place to live—a slave shack—and a job in his fields at low wages. What would you do?

____

____

____

____

____

____

4. You are a woman sent to the South after the Civil War to teach at a school for Black children. Last night you received a warning from a vigilante group that your life was in danger if you continued. What would you do?

____

____

____

____

Name: ______________________ Date: ______________

The First Reconstruction Act

To launch its new Reconstruction plan, Congress passed the first Reconstruction Act on March 2, 1867, in spite of President Johnson's veto.

The act nullified all Southern state governments and divided the Confederacy into five military districts, each ruled by a military governor appointed by Congress.

The Reconstruction Act of 1867 nullified all Southern state governments and divided the Confederacy into five military districts, each ruled by a military governor appointed by Congress.

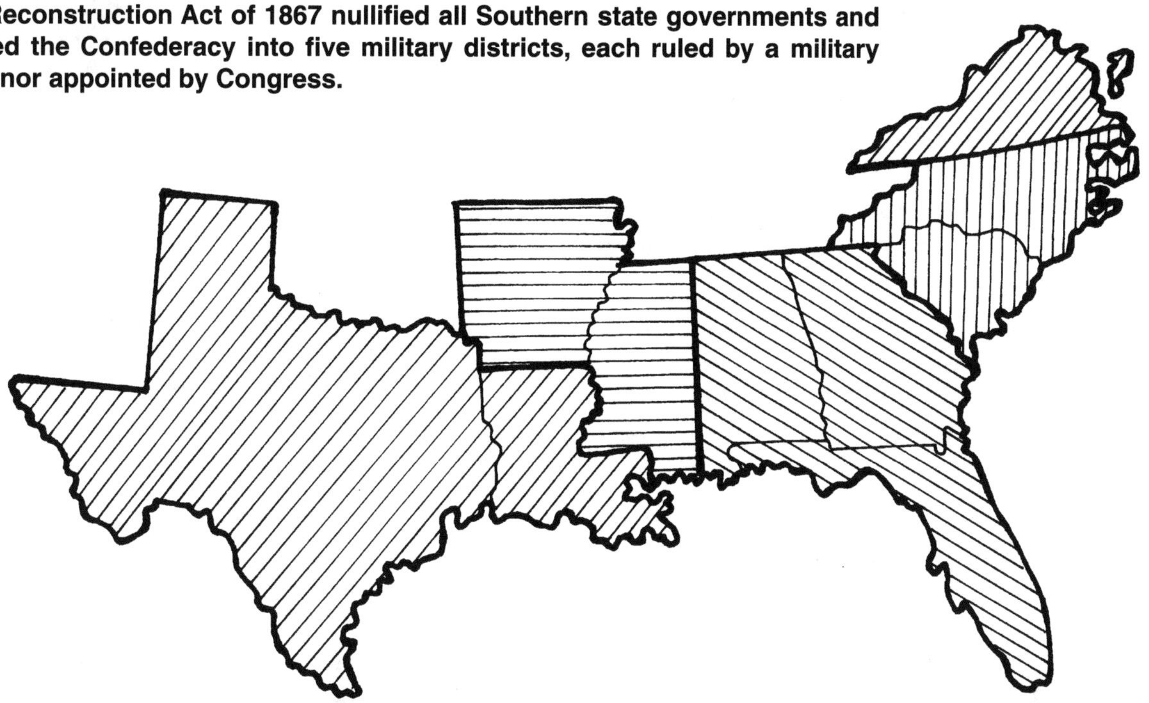

"The whole fabric of Southern society must be changed," stated Thaddeus Stevens.

The Act stated that the Southern states were to remain under federal military control until they were readmitted to the Union.

The Reconstruction Act also called for new state elections. Former Confederates were not allowed to vote or hold office. To ensure that Blacks were permitted to vote, Union soldiers were sent into the South to maintain law and order. In spite of resistance by Whites, 16 freedmen were elected to Congress.

1. What do you think Stevens meant? ______________________

2. Do you agree or disagree? Why? ______________________

3. If you had been a White Southerner, how would you have felt about this? Explain on your own paper.

Name:____________________ Date:____________

The Tenure of Office Act

Although President Johnson vetoed the bill, Congress passed the Tenure of Office Act on March 2, 1867. The Tenure of Office Act denied the president the power to remove anyone from office who had been appointed with the consent of the Senate unless the Senate agreed.

Radical Republicans hoped that this would prevent President Johnson from replacing Secretary of War Edwin Stanton, who favored their Reconstruction Plan.

Cabinet members are appointed by the president and approved by Congress. Their job is to act as advisors to the president. President Johnson claimed that the act was unconstitutional because it interfered with the executive powers of the president included in the Constitution.

Edwin Stanton

In August 1867, Johnson fired Edwin Stanton and appointed Ulysses S. Grant in his place. Grant had ambitions to run for president in the next election. He was warned that he might lose his chance to be nominated if he continued as secretary of war.

Grant resigned after five months and returned the position to Edwin Stanton, who barricaded himself in his office in the War Department. Johnson ordered his removal and appointed General Lorenzo Thomas to the position.

Congress began impeachment proceedings against President Johnson to have him removed from office. His violation of the Tenure of Office Act was the main charge against him.

Most of the Tenure of Office Act was repealed 20 years later. In 1926, the Supreme Court declared the act unconstitutional.

1. Use a dictionary. Define *tenure*. ____________________

2. Do you think it was fair to make it illegal for a president to fire someone he had appointed? Why or why not?

3. If you had been Grant, what would you have done? ____________________

Name: ______________________________ Date: ______________

More Reconstruction Acts

Rather than accepting the provisions of the first Reconstruction Act and rewriting their constitutions, most Southern states ignored the law. No attempts were made to change their state constitutions or to reapply for admission to the Union.

For this reason, Congress passed three additional Reconstruction Acts. President Johnson vetoed each one, but they were passed anyway.

The Reconstruction Act of March 1867 allowed military commanders to control registration and voting. They were given the power to force states to call conventions to revise the state constitutions to conform with federal requirements. As a result, many freedmen were elected to local offices and became active members of the conventions.

The third Reconstruction Act passed in July added a provision that the Fifteenth Amendment must be ratified before the Southern states could be readmitted to the Union.

However, the Fifteenth Amendment and the new state constitutions had to be ratified by a majority of registered voters. To prevent this, Southerners simply refused to vote.

Congress passed a fourth Reconstruction Act in March 1868 stating that a majority of the votes actually cast would decide the adoption or rejection of a state constitution.

1. Why do you think President Johnson vetoed all of the Reconstruction Acts?

____

____

____

____

2. Give an example to explain the difference between "the majority of registered voters" and "the majority of votes actually cast."

____

____

____

____

____

3. Why do you think Southerners refused to accept the Reconstruction acts and abide by them?

____

____

____

____

____

Name: ____________________ Date: ____________

The Fifteenth Amendment

Although the Fourteenth Amendment gave Black men all rights of citizenship, many Blacks were denied those rights, particularly the right to vote. Congress felt it was necessary to add another amendment that very specifically stated that all citizens had the right to vote and that no state could deny that right.

In many Southern states, particularly in Louisiana and Georgia, illegal methods were used to prevent former slaves from voting. Many were "disqualified" as voters by local officials. Terrorism by groups like the Ku Klux Klan frightened many potential Black voters and kept them away from the polls.

☆☆☆☆☆☆☆☆☆☆☆☆☆☆☆☆☆☆☆☆☆☆☆☆☆

Amendment 15

Section 1. The right of citizens of the United States to vote shall not be denied or abridged by the United States or by any state on account of race, color, or previous condition of servitude.

☆☆☆☆☆☆☆☆☆☆☆☆☆☆☆☆☆☆☆☆☆☆☆☆☆

Proposed in February 1869, the Fifteenth Amendment was ratified in March of the following year. Section 2 gave Congress the right to make laws to enforce this amendment.

Since the Fourteenth Amendment defined citizens as males over the age of 21 except for Native Americans, the right to vote was still denied to women. Women's **suffrage**, (the right to vote) became a major issue during Reconstruction and was not finally resolved until the Nineteenth Amendment was passed in 1920.

Many places in the South ignored the amendments and continued to prevent Blacks from exercising their rights. As late as 1965, Congress still felt it necessary to pass the Voting Rights Act.

1. How would you have felt if you were a Black man in the South who was prevented from voting by local officials?

____

____

____

____

2. How do you think women felt when former male slaves, most of whom could not read or write, were allowed to vote, while all women, even those who were well educated, were not allowed to vote?

____

____

____

Name: ______________________________ Date: ______________

Conduct an Interview

You are a reporter for a Northern newspaper in 1870. Your boss sent you to write an article about Reconstruction in the South.

He wants you to interview a former slave or a former slave owner. Which would you rather interview? ______________________________

Write 12 questions you could ask that person during an interview.

1. ______________________________
2. ______________________________
3. ______________________________
4. ______________________________
5. ______________________________
6. ______________________________
7. ______________________________
8. ______________________________
9. ______________________________
10. ______________________________
11. ______________________________
12. ______________________________

Name: ______________________________ Date: ______________

Reconstruction Era Trivia

- "Forty Acres and a Mule"—this expression came to symbolize the expectations of newly-freed slaves based on promises that Congress would divide up Southern estates and give them to former slaves. The expression came to mean any expectations that were unreasonable.
- As a member of the Tennessee State Legislature, Andrew Johnson refused to approve funds for a railroad, claiming that it would frighten horses.
- President Grant was arrested once while he was president and fined $20 for exceeding the speed limit. He was riding his horse at the time.
- President Andrew Johnson offered a reward of $100,000 for the capture of Jefferson Davis. In today's dollars, that would be the equivalent of over one million dollars.
- Both of Ulysses S. Grant's parents were alive when he became president. That was the first time in history it had happened to any president.
- When Andrew Johnson died, he left no will. His last written request was: "When I die, I desire no better winding sheet than the Stars and Stripes, and no softer pillow than the Constitution." His body was wrapped in an American flag, and a copy of the Constitution was placed beneath his head in his coffin.
- Mr. and Mrs. Grant were invited to attend the theater with President and Mrs. Lincoln on April 14, 1865. They were unable to attend. That night Lincoln was assassinated.
- Due to poor health, Eliza Johnson was not an active first lady. Her daughter, Martha Patterson, ran the domestic affairs at the White House and acted as hostess on social occasions.

- To provide the First Family with fresh milk and butter, Martha Patterson, the Johnsons' daughter, bought two cows and let them graze on the White House front lawn.

- The marble used to build Grant's tomb came from Montello, a small town in Wisconsin.

1. Use reference sources. Write two other interesting bits of Reconstruction Era Trivia.

____

____

____

____

Name: ______________________________ Date: ______________

Carpetbaggers

Government agents, politicians, businessmen, adventurers, and others from the North who traveled to the South during the Reconstruction period were called **carpetbaggers**.

The name came to be used because people who traveled often carried their belongings in carpetbags. Carpetbags were similar to today's sports bags—soft-sided suitcases, made of carpeting with wooden handles.

Some carpetbaggers were representatives of the Freedmen's Bureau and other federal Reconstruction agencies. They were not well received by White Southerners.

Many of the people who became active in the South during Reconstruction included Black and White teachers from the North and South and people from missionary organizations, churches, and schools. Their goal was to improve living conditions and to promote education for the freedmen.

Others were opportunists, looking for ways to exploit the political and financial problems of the South for their own gain. Because Congress banned all former Confederate leaders and soldiers from voting or holding public office for a time, carpetbaggers were often able to get elected.

Some carpetbaggers did benefit financially or politically during Reconstruction. Many others were able to improve education, provide medical assistance, and help restore Southern cities. Southerners who cooperated with carpetbaggers were called **scalawags**.

1. Why do you think White Southerners did not want representatives of government agencies in the South?

____

____

____

2. How do you think White Southerners felt about the teachers and missionaries who came to the South?

____

____

____

3. Use a dictionary to define *scalawag.* ______________________________

____

4. How do you think White Southerners felt about scalawags? ______________________________

____

____

Name: ______________________________ Date: ______________

Cause and Effect

A **cause** is an event that produces a result. An **effect** is the result produced. For each effect, write a possible cause.

Cause	Effect
______________________	1. Andrew Johnson was selected to run with Abraham Lincoln in the 1864 Presidential election.
______________________	2. Congress passed many Reconstruction Acts that President Johnson had vetoed.
______________________	3. Andrew Johnson did not run for re-election as president.
______________________	4. Ulysses S. Grant was elected president in 1868.
______________________	5. The first Civil Rights Act was passed in 1866.
______________________	6. Three new amendments were added to the Constitution after the Civil War ended.
______________________	7. Violence erupted in many places in the South during the Reconstruction Era.

Name: ______________________________ Date: ______________

Different Points of View

Reconstruction was one of the most controversial periods in American history. To learn what happened and why, it helps to read and consider more than one point of view.

Here are two different points of view:

A. President Johnson interfered with reasonable proposals for Reconstruction by using the power of the presidential veto. He wanted to allow the South to return to the way it was before the war.

B. President Johnson tried to keep Congress from passing vengeful measures against the South at a time when they needed to return to a normal life as soon as possible.

1. History is the true story of events that took place in the past. Everyone reporting on an event will report the same facts. Do you agree or disagree? Why?

____

____

2. Write one sentence about Reconstruction from the point of view of each group of people.

Southern leaders and former slave owners: ______________________________

____

____

Former Confederate soldiers: ______________________________

____

____

Former Union soldiers: ______________________________

____

____

Freed slaves: ______________________________

____

____

Blacks who lived in the North: ______________________________

____

____

Poor Whites who lived in the South: ______________________________

____

____

Name:______________________________ Date:______________

The Impeachment of the President

On February 24, 1868, the House of Representatives voted 126 to 47 to impeach Andrew Johnson for "high crimes and misdemeanors." Eleven charges were brought against Johnson. Eight of the charges were for violating the Constitution.

Johnson would now have to stand trial in the Senate to see if he would be removed from office. No U.S. President had ever been impeached before.

Johnson exploded when he heard the news. "Damn them! Haven't I been struggling ever since I have been in this chair to uphold the Constitution they trample underfoot!"

The trial began on March 23, 1868. Day after day evidence was presented and witnesses called. The case against the president was weak, based more on hatred and emotion than on fact. Johnson was represented by lawyers and did not attend the trial.

On May 7, 1868, the 54 members of the Senate on the jury began to weigh the evidence. They needed a two-thirds majority—36 votes—for a conviction. If only 35 voted guilty, Johnson would be acquitted.

The decisions of all members of the jury except one were known in advance. Senator Edmund Ross of Kansas remained undecided. The Radical Republicans put pressure on him and even attempted to bribe him.

On May 16, each member of the jury was asked how he voted. Senator Ross's vote was critical. One more vote was needed for a majority to convict the president and remove him from office.

Although he knew his political career would probably be over, Senator Ross voted not guilty. By a margin of one vote, the president was not convicted.

Andrew Johnson finished out his term as president. He and Congress continued to be at odds. Johnson continued to veto bills he thought were unfair.

"Everyone misunderstands me," Johnson claimed. "I am not trying to introduce anything new. I am only trying to carry out the measures towards the South that Mr. Lincoln would have done, had he lived."

1. Use a dictionary. Define *impeach.* ______________________________

____

2. Use reference sources. What other president was impeached? ______________

3. Was he found guilty or not guilty? ______________________________

Name: ______________________ Date: ____________

Matching

Place the letter of the statement from the right next to the corresponding term on the left.

_____ 1. abolish

_____ 2. amendment

_____ 3. Black Codes

_____ 4. carpetbaggers

_____ 5. civil rights

_____ 6. emancipation

_____ 7. impeach

_____ 8. Ku Klux Klan

_____ 9. ratified

_____ 10. Reconstruction

_____ 11. scalawag

_____ 12. suffrage

_____ 13. vagrant

_____ 14. veto

_____ 15. vigilantes

A. Freedom from slavery

B. People or groups who take the law into their own hands and punish others without a trial

C. A citizen's rights to vote, assemble, due process, etc.

D. An organization of Whites that used violence and terror to keep Blacks from exercising their civil rights

E. To officially end something

F. To charge with a crime

G. People from the North who became leaders in the South during Reconstruction

H. A change or addition to the Constitution

I. The right of a president to refuse to sign a bill passed by Congress to keep it from becoming a law

J. The right to vote

K. A person who has no home or means of support

L. Approved

M. A term used by many Southerners to describe people who supported the North's Reconstruction plan

N. Laws passed in the South to keep Blacks from exercising their civil rights

O. Rebuilding

Name: ______________________________ Date: ______________

Ulysses S. Grant Grows Up

The oldest of six children, Ulysses S. Grant was born in a two-room cabin in Ohio. A year later, Grant's parents moved to Georgetown, Ohio. Upon their arrival, his father, who was a tanner, built the family a modest brick home on a small piece of farmland; across the street he built a tannery.

Grant's education began in a one-room schoolhouse when he was five. His best subject in school was arithmetic.

Grant disliked the work and smells of the tannery business; however, he did enjoy anything to do with horses. From the time he was seven or eight years old, his job was to use the horses to haul wood to the house and tannery.

By the time he was 11, Grant did all the work on the farm that required the use of horses—plowing, furrowing, planting, and bringing in the harvest.

By the time he was 11, Grant did all the work on the farm that required the use of horses—plowing, furrowing, planting, and bringing in the harvest.

After Grant attended one year at the Presbyterian Academy when he was 16, Grant's father asked his friend Congressman Thomas Hamer to recommend his son for West Point Military Academy. Although he was reluctant to attend because "A military life had no charms for me …," Grant began at West Point in May 1839.

Somehow at West Point, the congressman had entered Grant's name incorrectly as "Ulysses Simpson Grant," rather than as Hiram Ulysses Grant. However, Ulysses Simpson Grant was the name he used for the rest of his life.

Grant didn't care much for the schoolwork at the Academy and didn't do very well in most subjects. However, in any course that involved horses, Grant excelled.

Use a dictionary.

1. What kind of work did a tanner do? ______________________________

   ____
2. What is a tannery? ______________________________

   ____
3. What is another word for arithmetic? ______________________________
4. Grant's father did not tell his son about attending West Point until after he had already been accepted. How do you think you would have felt about that if you had been Grant?

   ____

   ____

   ____

Name: ______________________________ Date: ________________

From Officer to Farmer to Clerk

Grant was the best horseman in his graduating class at West Point. When he graduated (21 out of 39), he hoped for an assignment in the cavalry. Instead, he became a second lieutenant in the infantry and was sent to St. Louis, Missouri, in 1843.

While stationed in St. Louis, Grant often visited a plantation owned by the parents of a classmate, Fred Dent. There, he met and fell in love with Fred's sister, Julia.

Because of trouble between Mexico and the United States in 1844, Grant's unit was notified that they would be sent south. Before he left, he asked Julia to marry him. Little did they realize that Grant would be gone for nearly four years fighting in the Mexican War.

Grant's skill with horses and bravery in battle earned him promotions and praise. He became the quartermaster for General Taylor's troops in Mexico.

Use a dictionary.

1. What is the infantry? ______________________________
2. What is the cavalry? ______________________________
3. What does a quartermaster do? ______________________________

____

Julia and Ulysses were married in August 1848 and spent the next four years at various outposts where he was stationed. Their first son, Frederick, was born in 1850.

When Grant was ordered to a post on the west coast, Julia could not join him because she was expecting another child. Grant found life boring in Oregon territory. He missed his family and began drinking heavily. After an incident when his commanding officer found him drunk in public, he demanded that Grant either resign or stand trial. Grant resigned, ending a 15-year military career.

Reunited with his family at last, Grant moved to land near St. Louis that Julia's father had given her. He cleared 60 acres for farming and built his family a home. Although he worked hard, Grant was not successful as a farmer. After a time, the only way he could support his family was by chopping and selling firewood.

Julia's cousin, Harry Boggs, hired Grant to work in his real estate business, but there too, Grant was a failure. Finally, his father offered him a job clerking in one of his leather goods stores in Galena, Illinois, but even at this job Grant did not do well.

Name: ______________________________ Date: ______________

Civil War Hero

When Lincoln called for volunteers to put down the "rebellion" in the South, Ulysses S. Grant was a 39-year-old clerk living in Galena, Illinois.

Grant decided to volunteer. "I thought I had done with soldiering. I never expected to be in military life again. But … if my knowledge and experience can be of any service, I think I ought to offer them."

Grant drilled other Galena volunteers and marched with them to Springfield. He wrote to the War Department requesting a military commission. His letter wasn't answered. When he went to Cincinnati to meet George McClellan, the General refused to see him.

About to return to Galena, Grant received word from the governor of Illinois offering him command of the Twenty-Fourth Illinois Volunteer Regiment and the rank of colonel. Grant proved himself a good officer. President Lincoln promoted him to Brigadier General. After his success in southern Illinois, Grant was sent to attack Confederate strongholds in Tennessee.

Grant became commander of the U.S. Army in the West following further victories. Under his leadership, the Union Army continued successful campaigns into the South, including the siege and capture of Vicksburg, Mississippi.

In March 1864, President Lincoln put Grant in charge of the entire Union Army. His goal was to capture the Confederate capital at Richmond, Virginia. With 118,000 troops, Grant directed the army south. During fierce battles, thousands were killed. After a siege of many months, Confederate General Robert E. Lee ordered a retreat. Finally on April 9, 1865, Lee surrendered to Grant near the village of Appomattox Court House, Virginia.

Learning that the Confederate troops had run out of food, Grant ordered supplies sent to them. When Union troops began loud celebrations, Grant ordered them to stop. "The war is over, the rebels are our countrymen again."

1. What other motives do you think Grant might have had when he volunteered besides serving his country?

   ____

   ____

2. Why do you think Grant was ignored when he first volunteered? ______________

   ____

   ____

3. Why do you think Grant did not let the Union troops celebrate loudly? ______________

   ____

Name: ______________________________ Date: __________________

Johnson or Grant?

Write a "G" on the blank if the statement refers to Ulysses S. Grant. Write a "J" on the blank if the statement refers to Andrew Johnson.

____ 1. As a boy, he was apprenticed to a tailor.

____ 2. He did well at any work that involved horses.

____ 3. He attended West Point Military Academy.

____ 4. He won his first election at the age of 19.

____ 5. He learned writing and arithmetic from his wife.

____ 6. He once ran away to avoid being arrested for a prank.

____ 7. He was arrested and fined for speeding.

____ 8. He fought in the Mexican War.

____ 9. He resigned from the army because of drinking problems.

____ 10. He served two terms as president.

____ 11. He served as vice president under Abraham Lincoln.

____ 12. His father was a tanner.

____ 13. He was elected governor of Tennessee.

____ 14. His wife's name was Eliza.

____ 15. His farm near St. Louis failed.

____ 16. He established Tennessee's first public school system and the state's first public library.

President Andrew Johnson

President Ulysses S. Grant

Name: ______________________________ Date: ______________

The Election of 1868

Other than the few months as the secretary of war under President Johnson, Ulysses S. Grant had never held any political office. In fact, he had never run for an election at any level.

When the Republican Convention met in 1868 to nominate a candidate for president, every delegate voted for Grant on the first ballot. Grant's running mate was Speaker of the House Schuyler Colfax of Indiana.

The Democrats nominated the governor of New York, Horatio Seymour, and Francis P. Blair of Missouri was chosen as his running mate.

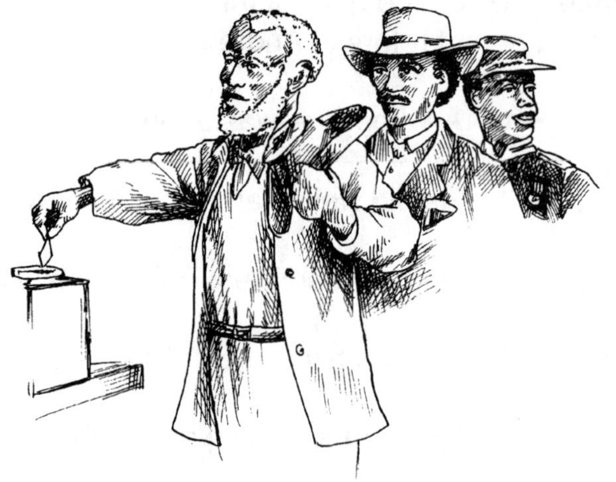

During the presidential campaign, the Democrats attacked the Reconstruction plan and Blacks' right to vote.

During the presidential campaign, the Democrats attacked the Reconstruction plan and Blacks' right to vote. They accused Grant of being a military despot and anti-Semitic. His running mate was accused of possible corruption.

The Republicans criticized Seymour's support for inflationary paper currency, Blair's reputed drunkenness, and Democratic opposition to Reconstruction.

Grant did not participate in the campaign. He remained at his home in Galena, Illinois, until the election results were known. Grant won the popular vote by 300,000 and earned 214 of the 294 electoral votes.

Many Blacks voted for the first time in that presidential election. Former Confederates, mostly Democrats, were denied the right to vote. These two circumstances helped Grant win.

In his inauguration address, Grant urged ratification of the Fifteenth Amendment and expressed concern for proper treatment of Native Americans. He felt that they, too, should be citizens and allowed to vote.

1. Why do you think the Republicans didn't nominate Andrew Johnson for reelection?

   ____

   ____

2. Why do you think Grant was nominated? ______________________

   ____

Use a dictionary.

3. What is a despot? ______________________________

   ____

4. What does *anti-Semitic* mean? ______________________

   ____

Name: ______________________________ Date: ______________

Grant's First Term

When Grant became president, he inherited many problems. Northern Republicans and Southern Democrats were still bitter rivals. Grant's lack of political experience soon became apparent. He appointed many personal and army friends to important positions.

Many of Grant's friends also lacked political experience and skills for the positions they received. Grant wasn't the first president to practice nepotism. Most civil service jobs were by appointment—from cabinet members to postmasters in small towns. Grant's loyalty was praised, but he was often criticized for his poor judgment.

As the states were readmitted to the Union, federal troops were withdrawn. The Fifteenth Amendment did grant Black men the right to vote; however, without federal protection, they were soon denied that right as well as many other civil rights in the South.

Terrorism and violence grew in the South. The Ku Klux Klan Act of 1871 gave Grant the authority to investigate and prosecute crimes. Over 1,000 men were convicted of terrorism.

William Seward, the man who negotiated the purchase of Alaska from Russia, proposed a plan for the Dominican Republic to become part of the United States. Grant was convinced that this was a good idea. The land was rich and had many mineral resources, an ideal place for settlements of newly-freed slaves. However, in spite of his strong support, Congress voted against the plan.

Another embarrassment to Grant occurred when two stock investors, Jay Gould and Jim Fisk, tried to corner the gold market by buying up gold to drive up the price. They pretended to be Grant's friends and convinced him not to sell any of the federal reserves of gold. When Grant realized what they were doing, he ordered $4 million in federal gold sold. That immediately lowered the price of gold and ruined Fisk and Gould's scheme, but it also caused financial ruin for many honest gold investors.

1. Why do you think it was not a good idea for Grant to appoint his friends to important positions?

   ____

   ____

   ____

2. Use an atlas. Locate the Dominican Republic.

   Do you think Grant's plan for the Dominican Republic would have helped solve some of the problems in the South? Why or why not?

   ____

   ____

   ____

3. Use a dictionary. Define *nepotism.* ______________________________

   ____

Name: ______________________________ Date: ______________

The Election of 1872

Near the end of Grant's first term as president, several important members of Congress were mixed up in a scandal involving stolen funds from the transcontinental railroad. Grant's vice president, Schuyler Colfax, and other government officials were accused of taking bribes.

Grant was not accused of any wrongdoing in the affair, and his popularity remained high. Again, he was nominated on the first ballot at the National Republican Convention. They did select a new running mate for his vice president, Senator Henry Wilson of Massachusetts.

Liberal Republicans decided to choose their own candidates. They nominated Horace Greeley, editor of the *New York Times,* and Governor B. Gratz Brown of Missouri. The Democrats supported Greeley also.

The campaign was filled with **mud-slinging**—personal accusations and insults against candidates. Political cartoons and insulting newspaper stories against Greeley were met with accusations of dishonesty, drunkenness, and stupidity against Grant.

Greeley supported civil service reform, a less radical approach to the South, and the end of Reconstruction. He toured the country giving speeches. At that time, it was unusual for a candidate to campaign for himself. Speeches were given by others but not by the candidates themselves.

The Republicans also called for civil service reform plus protection of Blacks' rights. Grant, knowing he was not a good public speaker, remained at the family home during the campaign. Grant won the popular vote by an overwhelming majority.

1. Why was "mud-slinging" an accurate term for what happened? ______________________

2. What do you think of mud-slinging as a way to run a campaign? ______________________

3. Do you think it is better for a candidate to campaign for himself or herself or to sit at home while others make the speeches? Why?

Name: ______________________________ Date: ______________

Scavenger Hunt

To complete this scavenger hunt, use the Internet and other reference sources to find the answers.

1. Joseph Hayne Rainey was the first Black American elected to the U.S. House of Representatives in 1870.

   What state was he from? ______________________

2. In 1870, another Black American, Hiram R. Revels, became the U.S. senator who replaced Jefferson Davis in Congress.

   What state was Revels from? ______________________

3. Following the Civil War, Southerners elected many former Confederate leaders, including the vice president of the Confederacy, to serve in the U.S. Congress.

   What was the name of the former vice president of the Confederacy? ______________________

4. President Lincoln invited Andrew Johnson to be his running mate in the 1864 presidential election.

   Who was Lincoln's vice president during his first term of office? ______________________

Hiram Revels being sworn in as a U.S. Senator

5. A holiday we still celebrate today was first celebrated nationally on May 30, 1868. Originally called Decoration Day, the day was set aside to decorate the graves of those killed in the Civil War.

   What do we call this holiday today? ______________________

6. What was Ulysses S. Grant's estate named? ______________________

7. Who was vice president when Andrew Johnson was president?

   ____

8. While Johnson was president, his secretary of state negotiated the purchase of Alaska from Russia for $7.2 million.

   Who was his secretary of state? ______________________

9. When Ulysses S. Grant ran for his second term of office, he received 286 electoral votes.

   How many electoral votes did his opponent, Horace Greeley, receive? ______________

Name:_______________________________ Date:_______________

Grant's Second Term as President

The *New York Tribune* described Grant's speech when he began his second term of office as "the utterances of a man of the best intentions profoundly desirous to govern wisely and justly and profoundly ignorant of the means of which good government is secured."

One scandal during Grant's administration involved officials of the Treasury Department responsible for collecting taxes on liquor. Known as the "Whiskey Ring," they failed to turn over some of the money they collected.

That prediction proved to be true as problem after problem plagued Grant's administration.

A severe drop in stock prices caused the Panic of 1873. Many banks failed and factories closed. The country faced a major economic depression.

Grant was unaware that he had appointed some unscrupulous men to work in his administration. They accumulated fortunes by selling business contracts, padding government payrolls, committing fraud, and taking bribes. Another scandal involved officials of the Treasury Department responsible for collecting taxes on liquor. Known as the "Whiskey Ring," they failed to turn over some of the money they collected.

Mrs. Grant wanted to have her sons closer to her. At her request, Grant appointed two of them as his personal secretaries. Again, people charged Grant with nepotism.

As his second term came to an end, Grant decided not to run again. (At that time there was no restriction on the number of terms for the president.) In his final State of the Union speech to Congress he said, "It was my fortune, or misfortune, to be called to the office of Chief Executive without any previous political training. Under such circumstances, it is but reasonable to suppose that errors of judgment must have occurred."

Grant did help the country survive the Reconstruction Era. He was the first president to try to help Native Americans and the first to use arbitration to solve international conflicts. He endorsed the Fifteenth Amendment and convinced Congress to pass the Ku Klux Klan Act, designed to protect the rights of Blacks.

1. Explain in your own words what the *New York Tribune* meant. Use a dictionary if you need help with any of the words.

____

____

____

____

2. On a scale of 1 to 10, with 10 being the best, how would you rate Grant as a president? Explain your answer on your own paper.

Name:______________________________ Date:_______________

True or False?

Circle "T" for True or "F" for False.

1. T F Andrew Johnson's plan for Reconstruction was much more radical than Abraham Lincoln's plan.
2. T F The Thirteenth Amendment outlawed slavery.
3. T F The Fourteenth Amendment gave everyone the right to vote including Blacks, women, and Native Americans.
4. T F The Fifteenth Amendment made organizations like the Ku Klux Klan illegal.
5. T F President Johnson and Congress agreed for the most part on plans for Reconstruction in the South.
6. T F Scalawags were people who left the South to find work in the North during Reconstruction.
7. T F Carpetbaggers were not popular in the South.
8. T F President Andrew Johnson was impeached.
9. T F Lincoln's Ten Percent Plan required that ten percent of the voters in a Confederate state must take an oath of loyalty to the United States.
10. T F The Freedmen's Bureau was formed to provide health care, education, and other benefits to former slaves.
11. T F No bill can become a law without the president's signature.
12. T F The Black Codes of 1865 and 1866 were passed by Congress to help Blacks in the South.
13. T F Majority means more than half.
14. T F The Tenure of Office Act denied the president the right to remove anyone from office who had been appointed with the consent of Congress.
15. T F Ulysses S. Grant was so popular he was elected president four times in a row.
16. T F President Johnson is the only president who was ever impeached.

Name: ______________________________ Date: ____________________

Read All About It!

Read a fiction or nonfiction book about the Reconstruction Era or a biography of someone who played a role in history at that time. A list of possible titles can be found on page 60.

Title and author of the book ______________________________

____

Was the book fiction or nonfiction? ______________________________

What years were covered in the book? ______________________________

Briefly describe the main character. ______________________________

____

____

Where did the main character live? ______________________________

____

Summarize two major events described in the book. ______________________________

____

____

____

____

____

____

What was the major problem the main character had to face? ______________________________

____

____

____

How was that problem resolved? If it wasn't resolved, why not? ______________________________

____

____

____

Did you like the book? Why or why not? ______________________________

____

____

Name: ______________________________ Date: ______________

Meet Rutherford B. Hayes

Use reference sources to learn about the man who became the nineteenth President of the United States.

Rutherford and Lucy Hayes

1. When and where was Hayes born? ____________
____
2. What does the B. in Rutherford B. Hayes stand for?
____
3. Hayes graduated from college at the age of 16 and then continued his education at Harvard. What college did he graduate from before Harvard?
____
4. After college, Hayes opened an office in Lower Sandusky, Ohio. What kind of office did he open?
____
5. Before becoming president, Hayes served three terms as governor of what state?
____
6. Hayes married his childhood sweetheart in December 1852. What was her name?
____
7. How many children did he and his wife have? ____________
8. Hayes fought in the Civil War. Did he fight in the Union or Confederate Army?
____
9. One of Hayes' nicknames was "Granny" Hayes because he didn't smoke, drink, or gamble. What was another of his nicknames?
____
10. First Lady Lucy Hayes did not serve liquor in the White House. What was her nickname?
____
11. How many terms did Hayes serve as president? ____________
12. What was the date of Hayes's death? ____________

Name: ______________________ Date: ______________

The Disputed Election of 1876

Although Ulysses S. Grant had been a popular president, his two terms of office were marred by scandals of bribery and corruption of public officials.

Since Grant had stated that he did not want to run for a third term, the Republicans nominated Rutherford B. Hayes. A moderate Republican, Hayes was not associated with any of the corruption of the Grant administration.

He too was a war hero, having risen to the rank of general and been wounded in the Civil War. Hayes was known for his honesty. As governor of Ohio, he had worked for civil rights for Blacks.

The Democrats nominated Samuel Tilden, governor of New York. He also had a reputation for honesty. He was backed by many wealthy businessmen.

Rutherford B. Hayes

Samuel Tilden

The election was close. When the votes were counted, Tilden had received 250,000 more votes than Hayes.

Presidential elections are not based on popular vote, however. The deciding factor is the number of electoral votes each candidate receives. Each state has a specific number of electoral votes, based on its population. To win the election, one candidate must have a majority of the electoral votes.

The Democrats claimed that votes from three Southern states (South Carolina, Florida, and Louisiana) had been falsely counted, and Tilden should have received those electoral votes. Both sides had used dirty tactics in the election, and both sides claimed victory in all three states. The electoral votes from those three states would decide the outcome of the election.

Congress set up an electoral commission of seven Republicans, seven Democrats, and Supreme Court Justice David Davis to settle the matter. Davis resigned from the commission and was replaced by a Republican. The committee gave the electoral votes of all three disputed states to Hayes, making him the winner 185 to 184.

On your own paper, answer the following questions.

1. Why do you think Hayes was a good choice for president?
2. How would you have felt about the electoral commission's decision if you had been a Democrat at that time?
3. Compare the election of 1876 to the election of 2000. List three similarities and three differences.

Name: ______________________________ Date: ______________

Hayes Becomes President

As Inauguration Day approached, the Democrats threatened to prevent the votes from being counted, and the election was still in dispute. Finally, a plan known as the Compromise of 1877 was reached.

The Democrats agreed not to block Hayes from becoming president if Hayes would agree to withdraw the remaining troops from the South, name a Southerner to the Cabinet, and approve federal funds to rebuild the South.

In the 1800s, if Inauguration Day fell on a Sunday, the new president had to wait until Monday to be sworn in. That was the case in 1877.

Grant's term of office officially ended on Sunday, March 4. Hayes wasn't scheduled to be sworn in until Monday, March 5, but Grant didn't want to take any chances of the country being without a president, even for one day.

The Grants invited several people, including Rutherford B. Hayes, to a farewell dinner at the White House on Saturday, March 3. After dinner, Grant invited Hayes and Morrison Waite, Chief Justice of the Supreme Court, to the Red Room. There, in secret, Hayes took the oath of office.

Use a dictionary.

1. Define *inauguration.* ______________________________

____

2. Define *compromise.* ______________________________

____

3. What is your opinion of the compromise? ______________________________

____

4. If you had been Samuel Tilden, how would you have felt about the compromise?

____

____

5. If you had been Rutherford B. Hayes, how would you have felt about the compromise?

____

____

6. Why do you think Grant was worried about the delay in swearing in Hayes?

____

____

Name: ________________________________ Date: ________________

Jim Crow Laws and Segregation

The Civil Rights Act of 1875 granted equal rights to Blacks in public accommodations. It made discrimination based on color illegal in theaters, hotels, and on railroads and gave Blacks the right to serve on juries.

However, that did not stop the South from passing segregation laws. The “Jim Crow” laws kept Blacks and Whites apart in public places like theaters, restaurants, hotels, schools, parks, trains, streetcars, and even restrooms and cemeteries.

“Jim Crow”

“Jim Crow” was a character invented by Thomas Rice for a song-and-dance routine in which he impersonated an old, crippled slave. Minstrel shows were popular entertainment in the early to mid 1800s. White actors made up to look like Blacks, sang, danced, and told jokes, most of which made fun of slaves.

After Reconstruction (from 1877 thereafter), Southern states passed laws requiring separation of Whites from “persons of color” in public transportation. Generally, anyone even suspected of having a Black ancestor was considered a “person of color.” Segregation not only separated the races, but it was also a way for Whites to achieve supremacy over Blacks.

Segregation was common in most public places and transportation. The goal of these laws was to prevent any contact between Blacks and Whites as equals.

Even the Supreme Court upheld the legality of Jim Crow Laws in a case in 1896, stating that segregation was legal if “separate, but equal” facilities were provided. (Most facilities were separate, but they were rarely equal.)

Laws were also passed to prevent Blacks from voting by imposing a poll tax—a fee charged at the voting booth that was too expensive for most Blacks to pay.

Many places also required voters to pass a literacy test to be eligible to vote. Since it had been illegal to educate slaves in the South, most adult freedmen could not read or write; therefore they could not vote.

Segregation was also practiced in the North. Although most states outlawed it after the Civil War, segregation was a reality in practice, if not in law.

1. Use a dictionary. Define *segregation.* ________________________________

   ____

2. How would you have felt if you were a Black and had to live in a state where Jim Crow laws were in effect? Write your answer on your own paper.

Name: ______________________ Date: ____________

Segregation Continues

Rather than getting more lax as time went on, the laws separating Whites and Blacks got stronger, and in some cases, very strange.

- In some cities, even in the North, it was illegal for a Black person to be within the city limits after sundown.
- A 1914 Louisiana law required separate entrances at circuses.
- Oklahoma passed a law in 1915 segregating telephone booths.
- It was illegal in Mississippi in 1920 to speak or write in favor of equality or marriage between Blacks and Whites.
- Arkansas required segregation at racetracks.
- Texas prohibited boxing matches between Whites and Blacks.
- Kentucky required that no textbook issued to a Black child would ever be reissued to a White school child and vice versa.
- In Florida, schoolbooks for Blacks had to be stored separately from those for Whites.
- In Alabama, it was illegal for Blacks and Whites to play checkers together.
- Georgia prohibited Black ministers from performing a marriage between two White people.

It took until 1954 for the Supreme Court to declare segregation in public schools unconstitutional. Some of the segregation laws remained in effect as late as 1964!

1. Interview someone you know who remembers when segregation was legal. On your own paper, write a short report about what you learned.

Segregation between Blacks and Whites involved many simple privileges as well, such as drinking from the same water fountain.

Name: ______________________________ Date: ______________

Success or Failure?

Was Reconstruction a success or a failure?

Some reasons why Reconstruction was a failure:

- In most places in the South, the rights granted to Blacks by the amendments and Civil Rights laws were ignored.
- Violence against Blacks increased.
- Although they legally had civil rights, in practice Blacks, especially in the South, were not much better off than they had been as slaves. They were free in name only.
- The North failed to control the South and to change the basic attitude of Southerners towards Blacks.
- Hard feelings between the North and South continued for many decades.
- The South continued to lag behind the North economically.

Some reasons why Reconstruction was a success:

- Three amendments were passed freeing slaves and giving them citizenship and the right to vote. At least in some parts of the country, Blacks were allowed their rights.
- Two Civil Rights Acts gave Blacks equality, at least in the eyes of the law.
- Even an unequal freedom was better than slavery.
- Although schools were segregated, and schools for Blacks were often less well-funded, the laws against education for Blacks had finally been repealed.
- Many people made a commitment to a society based on equality. Even though it did not become a reality during Reconstruction, the groundwork for future change and the Civil Rights movement of the nineteenth century was established.

1. What do you think? Was Reconstruction more of a failure or a success?

____

____

____

____

____

____

____

____

Name: ________________________________ Date: ________________

Then and Now

Read the statements about conditions during Reconstruction. Add a statement about conditions today.

Then: In the early years after the Civil War, the Black Codes kept Blacks in the South in conditions close to slavery.

Now: ____

____

Then: Even though the Civil Rights Act of 1875 gave Blacks equal rights in public places like hotels, trains, and theaters, they were seldom able to exercise those rights.

Now: ____

____

Then: After they were free, Blacks in the South were denied their rights. Even in the North, they faced much prejudice.

Now: ____

____

Then: Andrew Johnson was President of the United States.

Now: ____

____

Then: The Radical Republicans controlled Congress. They were engaged in what was almost an open war with the president.

Now: ____

____

Then: Women and Native Americans were not considered citizens and were not allowed to vote.

Now: ____

____

Name: ______________________________ Date: ______________

What Happened When?

Use the time line on page 2. Number these events in order from 1 to 13, with 1 being the event that happened first.

A. _____ Ulysses S. Grant became president.

B. _____ Rutherford B. Hayes became president.

C. _____ Andrew Johnson became president.

D. _____ Congress passed the first Civil Rights Act.

E. _____ Congress established the Freedmen's Bureau.

F. _____ Arkansas, Alabama, Florida, Louisiana, and North and South Carolina were readmitted as states.

G. _____ The United States purchased Alaska from Russia.

H. _____ The Fourteenth Amendment passed.

I. _____ The amendment abolishing slavery was passed.

J. _____ Georgia, Mississippi, Texas, and Virginia were readmitted as states.

K. _____ Congress voted to impeach President Johnson.

L. _____ Congress passed the first Reconstruction Act.

M. _____ The Fifteenth Amendment passed.

1. List two important historical events that occurred before the Reconstruction Era.

____

____

____

2. List two important historical events that occurred after the Reconstruction Era.

____

____

____

Name: ______________________________ Date: ________________

What Else Happened?

For each year, write one historical event that occurred in the United States that was unrelated to Reconstruction.

1865 ______________________________

____

1866 ______________________________

____

1867 ______________________________

____

1868 ______________________________

____

1869 ______________________________

____

1870 ______________________________

____

1871 ______________________________

____

1872 ______________________________

____

1873 ______________________________

____

1874 ______________________________

____

1875 ______________________________

____

1876 ______________________________

____

1877 ______________________________

____

Reconstruction Projects

Select one of these ideas for a project. Work alone, with a partner, or with a small group if appropriate.

1. Create a detailed time line of the Reconstruction Era with illustrations and maps.
2. Make a videotape of an interview with a former slave.
3. Make a videotape of an interview with a former slavemaster.
4. Write and perform a short play about conditions in the South during Reconstruction.
5. Write a detailed report about the accomplishments of the Freedmen's Bureau. Include specific examples.
6. Do a detailed comparison between Abraham Lincoln and Andrew Johnson. Include ways in which they were alike and ways in which they were different.
7. Make a scrapbook about the Reconstruction Era. Add captions for all pictures. You can download pictures from the Internet, photocopy them from books, or draw your own.
8. Write articles for one page of a newspaper dated any time between 1865 and 1877.
9. Write and illustrate a poem about the Reconstruction Era from the point of view of a freed slave. Read your poem to the class.
10. Research the charges against Andrew Johnson. Select one person to present the charges and one to defend the president. Take a class vote. Remember, it takes a two-thirds majority for the president to be removed from office.
11. Make a carpetbag.
12. Write a detailed report about the conditions in one Southern city or town during the Reconstruction Era.
13. Create a journal that could have been written by a freed slave between January 1, 1865, and December 31, 1877. Include at least five entries for each year.
14. Prepare and present a ten-minute speech you might have given if you had been a moderate member of Congress in 1866.

Learn More About …

Learn more about one of the people or groups listed below who had an impact on history during the Reconstruction Era. Use the Internet and other reference sources to write a three- to five-page report. Add illustrations and maps if appropriate.

William Seward

Blanche K. Bruce

Francis P. Blair
B. Gratz Brown
Blanche K. Bruce
Schuyler Colfax
Kate Cumming
Frederick Douglass
W.E.B. DuBois
Oscar J. Dunn
William Evart
Jim Fisk
Nathan Forest
Jay Gould
Julia Dent Grant
Ulysses S. Grant
Horace Greeley
Lucy Webb Hayes
Rutherford B. Hayes
Oliver Howard
Julia Ward Howe
Andrew Johnson
Eliza McCardle Johnson
Knights of the White Camelia
Ku Klux Klan
Abraham Lincoln
John W. Menard
Ely S. Parker
Joseph Hayne Rainey
Hiram R. Revels
Carl Schurz
William Seward
Horatio Seymour
Robert Smalls
Edwin Stanton
Thaddeus Stevens
Charles Sumner
Samuel Tilden
Benjamin Wade
Henry Wilson

Eliza McCardle Johnson

Julia Dent Grant

Read More About the Reconstruction Era

Nonfiction:

The Road to Freedom: A Story of the Reconstruction by Jalari Asim

Ulysses S. Grant by Lucille Falkof

Lincoln: A Photobiography by Russell Freedman

Abraham Lincoln: President of a Divided Country by Carol Green

Reconstruction and Reform by Jay Hakim

The Black Man in America: 1861–1877 by Florence Jackson

Reconstruction by Brendan January

An Album of Reconstruction by William Loren Katz

Reconstruction and National Growth by William Loren Katz

Andrew Johnson by Zachary Kent

Ulysses S. Grant by Zachary Kent

Lincoln and the Emancipation Proclamation by Frank B. Latham

The Rise and Fall of "Jim Crow" 1885–1964 by Frank B. Latham

Freedom Comes to Mississippi: The Story of Reconstruction by Milton Meltzer

Reconstruction: America After the Civil War by Zak Mettger

Reconstruction: The Great Experiment by Allen W. Trelease

Fiction:

Be Ever Hopeful, Hannalee by Patricia Beatty

I Thought My Soul Would Rise and Fly: The Diary of Patsy, a Freed Girl, Mars Bluff, South Carolina, 1865 by Joyce Hansen

Out From this Place by Joyce Hansen

The Heart Call Home by Joyce Hansen

Which Way Freedom? by Joyce Hansen

Changes for Addy by Connie Porter

Forty Acres and Maybe a Mule by Harriet Robinet

Answer Keys

Lincoln's Ten Percent Plan (page 5)
1. 100,000

The Thirteenth Amendment (page 6)
1. Emancipation: freedom from slavery
3. 75%

Andrew Johnson's Early Life (page 7)
1. Apprentice: learner of a trade
2. Tailor: a person who sews clothing

Learn More About Andrew Johnson (page 10)
1. Johnson was born in Raleigh, North Carolina, on December 29, 1808.
2. The boys rocked an old woman's little house back and forth on its foundation.
3. William
4. Five: Martha, Charles, Mary, Robert, and Andrew, Jr.
5. Military governor of Tennessee
6. It was turned into a barracks for Confederate soldiers.
7. George Atzerodt
8. After failing to be elected to Congress in 1869 and 1872, Johnson was elected to the U.S. Senate in 1875.
9. He died at his daughter's home in Carter County, Tennessee, on July 31, 1875, following a stroke.

Reconstruction Under President Johnson (page 11)
1. Freedman: a former slave

Black Codes of 1865 and 1866 (page 12)
1. Vagrant: a person without a home or job

The Freedmen's Bureau (page 14)
1. Veto: the right of the president to refuse to sign a bill to prevent it from becoming a law

How Congress Passes Laws (page 15)
1. U.S. Constitution
2. bill
3. majority
4. ten
5. two-thirds

The Congressional Plan (page 20)
1. Majority: more than half
2. 500,001

Tenure of Office Act (page 28)
1. Tenure: a guarantee of a job to protect a person from being fired

More Reconstruction Acts (page 29)
2. Example: If there were one million registered voters in a state, a majority of registered voters would equal 500,001. However, if there were one million registered voters and only 500,000 actually voted, a majority of votes cast would equal 250,001.

Carpetbaggers (page 33)
3. Scalawag: a rogue; a scamp. When applied by Southerners during Reconstruction, the term had a very negative connotation.

The Impeachment of the President (page 36)
1. Impeach: to formally charge a person in a political office with a crime
2. William J. Clinton
3. Not guilty

Matching (page 37)

1. E	6. A	11. M
2. H	7. F	12. J
3. N	8. D	13. K
4. G	9. L	14. I
5. C	10. O	15. B

Ulysses S. Grant Grows Up (page 38)

1. Leather work; a tanner cures hides and/or makes items of leather
2. A place where hides are cured and worked to make leather
3. Mathematics

From Officer to Farmer to Clerk (page 39)

1. Infantry: foot soldiers
2. Cavalry: mounted soldiers
3. Quartermaster: an officer who deals with supplies. In Grant's time, the position also included being in charge of the packhorses and mules that carried the supplies.

Johnson or Grant (page 41)

1.	J	7.	G	12.	G
2.	G	8.	G	13.	J
3.	G	9.	G	14.	J
4.	J	10.	G	15.	G
5.	J	11.	J	16.	J
6.	J				

The Election of 1868 (page 42)

1. Despot: a dictator
2. Anti-Semitic: anti-Jewish

Grant's First Term (page 43)

3. Nepotism: appointing friends and family members to important positions

Scavenger Hunt (page 45)

1. South Carolina
2. Mississippi
3. Alexander Stephens
4. Hannibal Hamlin
5. Memorial Day
6. Mount McGregor
7. No one. Johnson did not have a vice president.
8. William Seward
9. None

True or False? (page 47)

1.	F	7.	T	12.	F
2.	T	8.	T	13.	T
3.	F	9.	T	14.	T
4.	F	10.	T	15.	F
5.	F	11.	F	16.	F
6.	F				

Meet Rutherford B. Hayes (page 49)

1. October 4, 1822, in Delaware, Ohio
2. Birchard
3. Kenyon College
4. A law office
5. Ohio
6. Lucy Ware Webb
7. They had eight children, seven boys and one girl. Three of their sons died in childhood.
8. Union
9. "His Honesty" or "Dark Horse President"
10. Lemonade Lucy
11. One
12. January 17, 1893

Hayes Becomes President (page 51)

1. Inauguration: a ceremony during which a public official takes office
2. Compromise: an agreement between two people or groups in which each one gives up something to settle a dispute

Jim Crow Laws and Segregation (page 52)

1. Segregation: separation to prevent one group from mixing with another

What Happened When? (page 56)

A.	10	H.	9
B.	13	I.	3
C.	2	J.	11
D.	4	K.	8
E.	1	L.	5
F.	7	M.	12
G.	6		